Paolo Macagno - Annalisa Bardella

GAMES FOR THE CLASSROOM

to play in the primary school
whilst having fun and improving
skills and abilities

for 6-11 year olds

DISTANCED GAMES
in accordance with COVID-19 guidelines

Giocando Si Impara
DCPM edizioni

This is dedicated to two special people
who are both excellent teachers and dear friends,
Leonarda Nacci and Luisa Perino

INTRODUCTION

These are games which can be played in the classroom whilst observing the distances recommended by the Covid-19 anti-contagion guidelines which are now obligatory in schools but can unfortunately compromise the global and social aspects of students' learning.

This publication is dedicated to those primary school teachers who, like us, consider games to be an integral part of learning and a cross disciplinary way to respond to the deeper needs of the child and his/her development. Theory and practice have demonstrated that, without a shadow of a doubt, groups games are the most natural and spontaneous way for children to grow, learn, test their limits and discover their talents.

In this book you will find 32 group games to use in the class-room (with pictures, photos and drawings) which are also linked to the primary curriculum. 5 of them could be considered essential "old classics" (*Fishing competition - Mime game - Team hangman - Name, object, place - Forbidden words*); whilst the other 27, while sometimes containing familiar elements of other games, have more original and unpublished formats.

These latter games arose from our daily research into finding a way to make school more lively and creative and to encourage students to participate and play an active role in their own learning, something which they have done with great enthusiasm and creativity (*Identity card - Find the word - How, where, when? - Art competition - Poetry competition - What or to what - The good and the bad - Question and answer - The circle of rhyme - The king orders - Guess which three - Guess what - The grandparents' dinner - The division challenge - Important things - The interview - Arithmetic Olympics - Hidden words or find the verb - Free words - Pass the paper - Mute painter - Point the finger - Sherlock Holmes - Yes or no - Rhythmic bingo – Auction - Full Schoolbag*).

The Russian linguist and anthropologist Vladimir Propp showed that fairy tales only have a limited number of "functions" (31 in fact) and we should bear in mind that this is also true for children's games. It is therefore only natural that we should find similarities between games from 100 years ago and today and games from children in Africa or any other continent.

Although the 32 games have been designed for use in the limited space available in a classroom, they are all "games" and, as such, all have the same characteristics of being adaptable, entertaining, functional, enjoyable and interactive. They allow children to release their emotions and interact, they are motivational, creative and empathetic whilst also helping the internalisation of those skills and concepts which are present in the school curriculum from Maths to English, and Music to Civil Education.

So whilst the scientific world is working to eradicate the virus which has us in the grip of a global pandemic, us teachers can also play our part by coming up with new ideas and strategies to deal with this new normality. We can find ways in which we can maintain the necessity of "physically social distancing" yet still take into consideration the needs of our youngest citizens to grow and develop skills and abilities on a global scale from working and playing in a group.

LIST OF GAMES

IDENTITY CARD

Materials: a felt-tip pen and a coloured piece of paper or card for every player, a board and marker pen or blackboard and chalk.

Background: every player writes a description of him/herself on the paper and the other players must recognise each participant through the characteristics described on the card.

How to play: this game focuses on our individual features and qualities, the awareness and respect for which is the basis for character development and physical and psychological well-being.

The participants can stay at their desks to play. Ideally divide the room into 2 parts thereby creating 2 teams one on the right and one on the left of the supervisor. Each team should choose a name (for example, the "the yellows" and "the blues" to match the colour of the cards used). In each team a "spokesperson" is appointed. The supervisor places the (black)board on a wall visible to all which will later be used as a scoreboard.

STEP ONE – COMPLETE YOUR IDENTITY CARD. Every player completes a kind of identity card about him/herself using the paper and felt-tip pen, following the prompts on the card below:

The 2 different pieces of coloured paper or card (one colour per team) should have been prepared by the supervisor and have enough space for the answers.

1	my favourite food
2	my favourite animal
3	my best quality
4	my 2 favorite colours
5	when i am grown up i want to be
6	my favourite film or TV series or cartoon
7	my favourite singer or group
8	what i think about school
9	my worst characteristic
name	

Once every player has completed his or her card he or she gives them to the supervisor.

STEP TWO - COMPARE AND GUESS. The supervisor randomly chooses one of the yellow identity cards and turns to the players of the blue team. The supervisor reads out the answer to question number 1 and gives the blue team a few seconds to discuss before the spokesperson for the blue team decides whether the supervisor should read the answer to question number 2 or if they are already ready to guess whose card it is from the yellow team.

If the blues guess the name of the owner of the identity card correctly after the first description they get 1 point (which the supervisor marks on the scoreboard), if they guess after the fifth description 5 points and if they still haven't guessed after the ninth clue, 9 points.

The supervisor alternates between reading one blue card and then one yellow card until all cards are finished. Obviously as the game progresses it will get easier to guess the identities of the owners of the cards from those who haven't already been picked. The winner is the team with the least points.

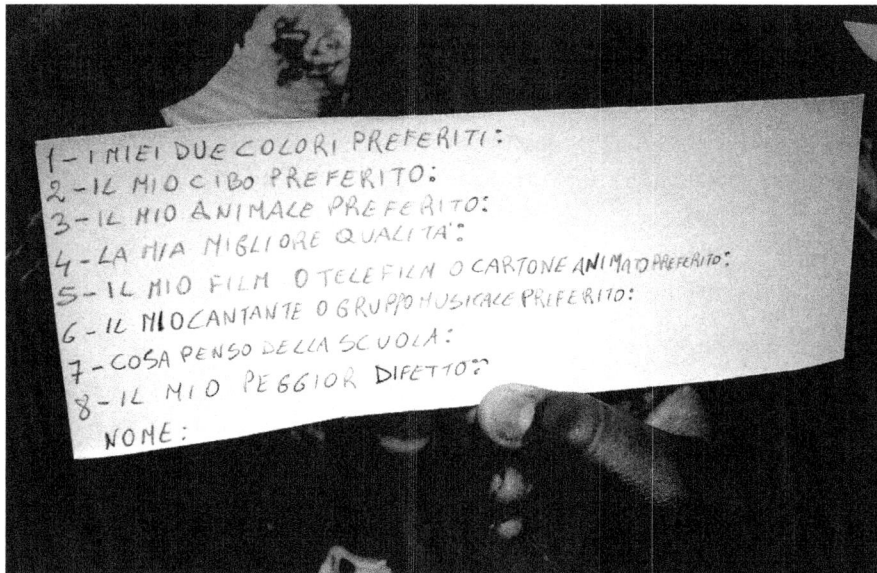

FIND THE WORD

Materials: one photocopied text for each student, a highlighter. In the variation coloured pencils are also required.

Background: players must identify the required words within a set time.

How to play: the supervisor gives each student a text of reasonable length (an extract from a story or a short story taken from a class book etc.) photocopied onto a normal sheet of A4 paper.

The instructions can vary depending on the level and age of the students. You can start by asking students to highlight all words containing the same syllable or words with accents etc. Or you could ask students to highlight all the definite articles, or common nouns, or verbs in the past simple etc. Or "derived names" etc.

When the allotted time has run out for each round players score a point for every word they have correctly identified.

Variation: using the same context we can ask students to highlight words to make a phrase which is completely different in meaning from the original text. They would therefore take an article, a noun, a verb, an adjective etc and try to compose as long a phrase as possible. In this case at the end of the allotted time each player reads out his/her phrase and if it is judged to be completely different from the original sense, he/she receives a point for every word used. A different coloured pencil should be used for each round in order to highlight the words necessary to make the new phrase. Words which have already been highlighted cannot be used again.

La leggenda del girasole

Un giorno, in un grande giardino in mezzo a tanti fiori colorati, era nato un fiore davvero strano: brutto e storto.

Tutti gli altri fiori dicevano che era il più brutto fiore fra tutti e nessuno voleva stargli vicino.

Il povero fiore, triste e solo, soffriva, ma non si lamentava mai. Trascorreva le sue giornate a guardare il sole nel cielo. Gli piaceva così tanto il sole che, per cercare di avvicinarsi a lui, si era allungato molto.

Quando il sole si spostava, anche il fiore lo seguiva girando la sua corolla. Un giorno il sole si accorse di quel fiore solo e triste che lo guardava sempre, decise di conoscerlo e gli si avvicinò.

Dopo aver ascoltato la triste storia del fiore, il sole decise di aiutarlo e con i suoi raggi splendenti abbracciò il fiore, che si accese subito di un bel giallo vivo e sembrava essere quasi d'oro. Da quel giorno il fiore diventò il più alto e il più bel fiore fra tutti quelli del giardino. Diventati amici, il sole decise che meritava un nome speciale e così da quel giorno venne chiamato GIRASOLE.

HOW, WHERE, WHEN?

Materials: a piece of paper, a pencil, a piece of red and green card for each player.

Background: couples take it in turns to compete against one another.

How to play: players sit at their desks at a suitable distance from each other. Each player puts their green card on the desk to show they are "in the game". The supervisor chooses the player to start the game.

The starting player chooses an object and, in order to guarantee fairness, writes its name on the piece of paper he/she has been given. Then he/she challenges one of his/her classmates to guess the object. The classmate can only ask 3 questions: "How do you use it?", "When do you use it?" and "Where do you use it?". From the three answers the classmate must try to guess which object it is and, if he/she guesses correctly, the starting player is eliminated (and has to put his/her red card on the desk). If the guess is not correct he/she is eliminated and must display his/her red card. Play continues until the final challenge between the last 2 students left in play.

11

ART COMPETITION

Materials: 2 identical sets of numbered A4 pieces of paper on which a few lines or shapes have been drawn (e.g. straight or curved lines, small and large geometric shapes etc.). In each set every sheet is different. A pencil rubber and pencil sharpener for every player.

Background: players are divided into 2 teams which represent the greatest artists from the 2 competing nations. Students try their hand at an individual test of drawing and creativity within a set time limit.

How to play: players remain at their desks. Divide the room into 2 teams each representing different nation (players can choose their nations).

Hand out the pieces of paper. Players should try to complete their drawing within a set time using the lines which are already on the sheet.

4 children (2 from each team) play the part of judges. They should be chosen from the front rows of desk so that, when it comes to voting, it is impossible for them to tell which drawing belongs to which player. The vote will therefore be fair and impartial.

When the time has run out the 2 drawings from sheet number 1, which had the same initial lines and shapes are compared, then number 2, number 3 etc (the sheets can be stuck to the wall with blu tack or tape). The 3 judges give points from 5 to 10 for each work of art. The supervisor records the individual votes. When all the pictures have been compared the individual points are counted up for the 2 teams.

POETRY COMPETITION

Materials: sheets of paper, pencils and pens or felt-tips.

Background: players impersonate budding writers taking part in a group poetry competition.

How to play: the supervisor asks the players to imagine they are writers and poets taking part in a poetry competition. Based on the layout of the desks they should form 4 groups, each group facing a different wall and with a large sheet of paper or board stuck to the wall in front of them where they can write with a large marker pen. Each group chooses someone to stand next to the board whilst the other players remain at their desks.

Players are now ready to form work groups competing against the other teams to write a poem or nursery rhyme within a set time limit.

The supervisor can choose a theme or topic for the poem based on the skills and level of the group or class or they can be given complete artistic licence to create whatever they want perhaps having previously read some nursery rhymes or poems for children in class.

The players sitting at their desks can have a pencil and paper to facilitate their creative work. The player at the board puts together the proposals of his/her teammates to create a complete work. The board should be used as a "rough copy" and so they shouldn't worry about scribbling or rubbing out on it.

At the end of the set time every player becomes a literary judge and should try to be completely impartial in their judging. The 4 poems are read out in turn and each poem is given a mark, the mark being the total of the votes from each team member (players vote by raising their hand and hold up their fingers from 1 to 5). Finally the winning team is applauded and praised and this is a good opportunity to make comparisons with the works of all the other groups.

12.02.2021

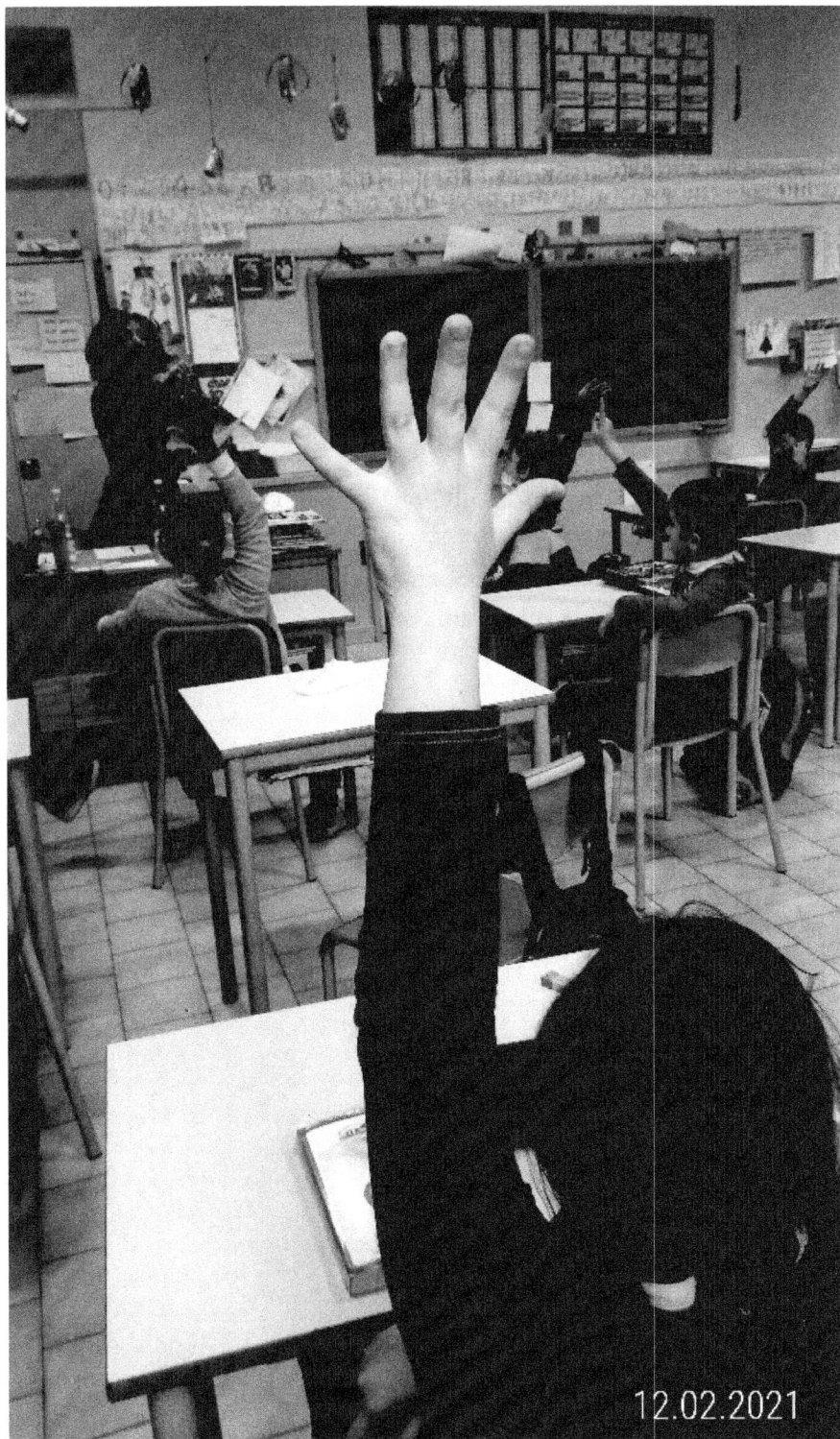

12.02.2021

WHAT OR TO WHAT

Materials: no materials are needed.

Background: players must guess a certain word or verb within a speech.

How to play: players can stay at their desks distanced from one another.

- TO WHAT. One player is chosen by the supervisor to stand up and, after being given a chance to think, to say a sentence in which the verb has been substituted by the verb "TO WHAT". For example: "Yesterday I went to the greengrocer TO WHAT tomatoes" instead of "to buy" (or even better "to look for" or "to take back"). After getting the hang of the game players will realise that to make it more difficult to guess the verb, they need to construct a phrase where there is the possibility to substitute many different verbs.

In every round the first person to guess the hidden verb stands up and invents the next phrase.

- WHAT. Following the same steps as above but with the substituted word being a "name of something/noun". In this case the child should produce a speech or monologue with appropriate pauses between one phrase and another (to think and listen to the suggestions of his/her classmates), in which he/she continues to substitute the word to be guessed until someone works out the word. For example: "at home yesterday I picked up a WHAT and I took it to school... then I ate the WHAT and it was really good... the WHAT was red... etc."

LO SO !

NON RIESCO A COSARE IL LAMPADARIO !

ANCHE IO !

IO LO SO !

THE GOOD AND THE BAD

Materials: no materials are needed.

Background: players must perform the correct action according to which category a chosen word fits into.

How to play: each player tucks his/her chair under and stands behind his/her desk. Desks should be clear of any materials and bags left outside the classroom.

The supervisor says one word at a time, choosing his/her words which could be classified as "good" or "bad" depending on what they are describing. Players respond to a "good" word by raising their arms (as if in joy) whilst for a "bad" word they should cover their ears with their hands (as if they don't want to hear).

They game should be played at a speed decided by the supervisor according to the demographics of the group.

For every new word, whoever gets the action wrong has to jump up and down 3 times on the spot, or, alternatively after 3 errors they can go to jail. At the end of the game everyone is praised but especially those who have avoided any kind of penalty.

Note: we strongly suggest reviewing the role and use of the "jail" in children's games with its function of "holding hostage" and then returning to the group. In the classic game "truth, dare, double dare, command, kiss, promise" the use of the jail, under the supervision of an adult to make sure that the actions are fun and rewarding, often requires, unsurprisingly, different skills from those in the original game and it performs the function of publicly redeeming the player who has been punished.

Variation: you can use the format of this game to create many variations by using 2 opposing categories which take 2 elements which can be compared with each other in some way. So the game could also be called "Odd and even" or "Proper nouns and common nouns", "Animal and vegetable", "Subjunctive or indicative" etc. You could later introduce the idea of 3 categories to compare e.g. "solid, liquid and gas" and naturally, in this case you would need to think of 3 different actions to represent the 3 concepts: for example for "table" players would stand with feet wide apart and arms folded, on the word "orangeade" players would crouch down with feet together and on the word "smoke" players would jump with their hands in the air.

QUESTION AND ANSWER

Materials: players' own desks and chairs.

Background: players compete in pairs.

How to play: each player tucks his/her chair under his/her desk and stands directly behind it. The desks should be clear of any materials and bags left outside the classroom.

One child is chosen by the supervisor to start the game and he/she chooses a classmate to challenge. The supervisor gives a word to the 2 challengers (for example "fish"). The 2 players have to quickly think of a question in their heads about fish (for example "what do fish use to breathe?" or "how does a fish rise to the surface or go deeper in the water?"). As soon as the players have got a clear question in their heads (which they should also know the answer to – an important detail to add at the start of the game) each child has to quickly run round his/her desk 2 or 3 times and then pull his/her chair out and sit down: the first player sitting wins the right to ask his/her opponent the question.

The winner is the person who manages to ask a question that his/her opponent can't answer (the supervisor can then check that the person who asked the question knows the answer) or if the question is answered correctly then that child is the winner.

Warning: in this game it doesn't always pay to be fastest. If players think of a question very quickly it is likely to be very simple and therefore the answer will be easy.

Whoever loses is temporarily excluded from the game until the next round. The number of couples will diminish until there is one couple left in the final round.

FISHING COMPETITION

Materials: a piece of squared paper or a notebook and a pencil, one per player.

Background: this is a team fishing competition where expert fishermen compete to see who can catch the most fish.

How to play: if possible divide the classroom into two halves and form 2 teams of fishermen. Each player draws a table 10 squares by 10 squares on his/her paper (which is the sea or a lake). Squared paper which is 1cm is ideal for this. The squares of the table are identified using coordinates corresponding to the rows and columns.

To start the game each player draws 4 fish of his/her choosing on the table: for example a pike of 4 squares, a carp of 3 squares, a trout of 2 and a chub of 1 square.

Players from each team take it in turns to cast their rods (as in the classic game of "battleships") giving 2 coordinates to indicate a precise square on the table. If a player from team A gives the coordinates of a square on which there is one or more fish (since more than one player may have chosen to draw their fish in the same position) all players from team A put a cross in the corresponding square: the fish has been captured and players don't need to guess any further squares for that fish (therefore there's no reason to choose an adjacent square in order to catch the rest of the fish). If there are no fish in that square players can put a zero to show that it is empty.

Play continues alternately between both teams until everyone has had a go. When all players have had 2 or 3 chances to cast their rods (depending on the number of players and time available) the number of fish caught is counted up.

The winners are the team who have caught the most fish.

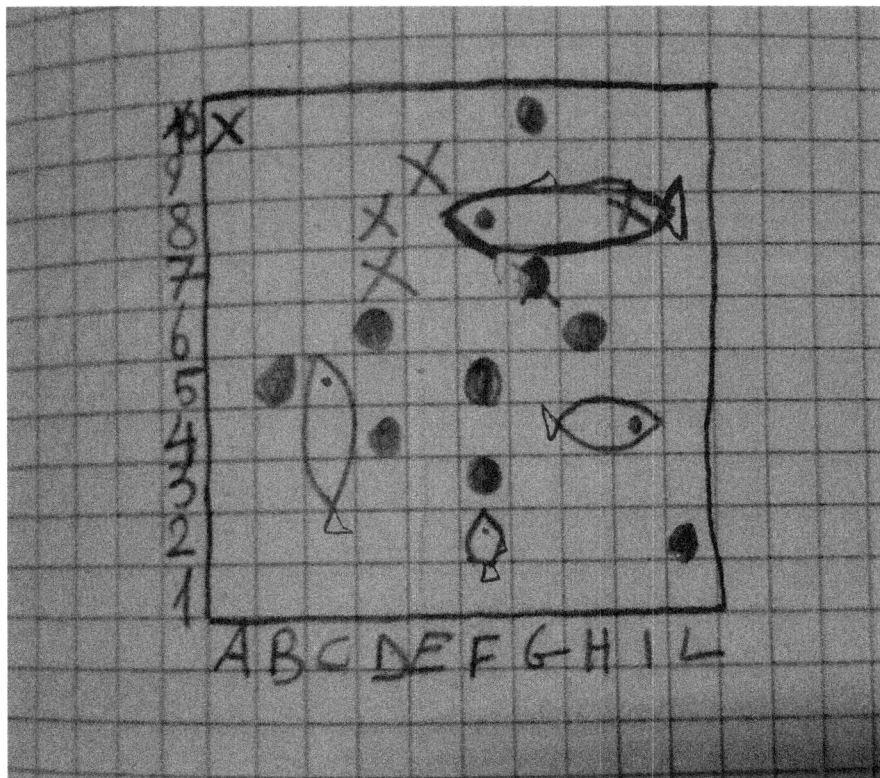

MIME GAME

Materials: an hourglass or stopwatch.

Background: players have to guess the action which one of their teammates mimes.

How to play: this is a very well-known game and is easy to set up. There are lots of variations.

After having chosen a category of words, for example ANIMALS or VERBS or JOBS etc. Players try to guess the chosen word which is being mimed.

In a simpler version one child mimes a word and whoever guesses the word first gets to mime the next one. The words to mime can be chosen beforehand by the supervisor or by each player on his/her turn.

In the version with 2 teams, the words which the first team come up with from a chosen category must be mimed and guessed by the second team (and vice versa) within a set time frame. Each word guessed correctly wins one point.

THE CIRCLE OF RHYME

Materials: no materials needed for players but the supervisor may use a whistle or bell.

Background: the game is a group game to see how many rhyming words players can come up with to correctly complete the "circle of rhyme".

How to play: each player sits at his/her desk or can stand or sit in a large circle. Players are given a number from 1 onwards excluding the supervisor.

Player number 1 gives the first word and number 2 "replies" with the first rhyming word, number 3 with the second word and so on. The supervisor's role is to make sure that players do not exceed the set time to complete the circle and to check on the correctness of the rhyme. When an incorrect "answer" is given, ie not in rhyme, the circle is interrupted and play starts again from player number 2 with a new word (play continues as players try to achieve the highest number of "circles of rhyme"). The game finishes when all players have suggested a word.

Each time the game is played, children should try to get a higher number of complete circles than the time before.

The whistle can be used by the supervisor to signal when the time has run out.

THE KING ORDERS

Materials: no materials needed.

Background: one player gives orders and the other players have carry out the orders or not.

How to play: this game is taken from the well-known game "Simon says".

Players stand in front of their desks and choose a classmate to be the temporary "leader" of the game. The "leader" gives orders one at a time in the style of a king who expects total obedience. Each order must be spoken in a clear voice and should refer to a movement, a gesture, a facial expression, a noise (which can be made with the voice or part of the body) that everyone is able to make. All the players in the circle must carry out the command immediately but only if the command is preceded by the phrase "the king orders you to…". So if the leader says "the king orders you to… raise your arms!" everyone should raise their arms or "the king orders you to… shout loudly!" everyone should shout; however if after this the leader says "move your shoulders!" or "the ring orders you to…" or "the king says…" or "and now… move your shoulders!" (whilst moving his/her own shoulders) this movement mustn't be carried out.

The objective of the game is for the "leader" to get the other players to carry out actions or make noises when he/she gives the command "the king orders you to…"; on the other hand he/she is also trying to get them to make mistakes by making actions, gestures, expressions or noises when he/she has not given the correct command or has missed it out entirely. The objective of the players is to carry out (or not) the king's orders exactly as the "leader" has said.

Whoever performs an action which has not been preceded by "the king orders you to…" is picked out by the leader (or the adult supervisor) and can continue to play or (according to the rules established before the game starts) must sit out the rest of the game until a new round starts.

During the game all players must be careful to carry out the orders to the letter since, for example if someone in the circle (including the "leader") in response to the order "the king orders you to… put your right hand on your left shoulder" does the action in reverse and uses the opposite hand and shoulder, this would be penalised according to the pre-established rules.

Every round of the game finishes when the "leader" a) makes a mistake - in which case he/she is substituted and all the eliminated players can join back in, or b) when he/she has managed to make all the players make a mistake, or c) when the time for each round has run out.

GUESS WHICH THREE

Materials: a small stone or pebble or a rubber or another small "token" for each player.

Background: for this game players should imagine that they are investigators on the verge of discovering the identity of 3 robbers who have stolen "3 gold coins from Queen Elizabeth" or "3 gold teeth from Father Christmas" or other similar plausible and amusing thefts.

How to play: each player can remain in his/her place with the token in his/her pocket. One of the players, chosen by the supervisor, goes out of the room. The supervisor chooses 3 children who each hold their token clenched tight in a fist and will be the "robbers". All other players should also put their tightly clenched fists out in front of them on their desks. The player outside the classroom comes back in and stands next to his/her desk. He/she then asks a question to each player in turn which can only be answered with YES or NO and may help him/her to guess the 3 robbers such as "has he/she got black hair?", "has he/she got glasses?", "has he/she got white shoes?" etc. (the questions should be about their appearance and the clothes they are wearing). The aim of the other players is to help the investigator so they should respond to his/her questions correctly whilst the 3 "robbers", when asked a question on their turn, can answer in a way so as to throw the investigator off the scent.

Once the investigator has completed one round of questioning he/she gives 3 names and unmasks the robbers. He/she checks if they have the "stolen goods": ie the token in their fist. If he/she has guessed correctly he/she wins the praise of his/her classmates and can choose who gets to be the investigator in the next round (otherwise the supervisor chooses).

Variation: we advise you to get familiar with the game by concentrating on questions limited to physical characteristics and clothing but as players gain in confidence the game can be made more entertaining (with older children) by expanding the areas of investigation to physical characteristics in a broader sense ("is he/she good at running?"... "does he/she eat a lot?"... "is he/she strong?" etc.) or to aspects of personality ("is he/she friendly?"... "is he/she kind?"... "is he/she a chatterbox?" etc.) or to tastes and opinions ("does he/she support

Turin?"... "does he/she love sport?"... "does he/she play an instrument?" etc.). With younger children it may be a good idea to start with one robber to guess, then two, and later three.

GUESS WHAT

Materials: everyday objects that students have at hand.

Background: an object is hidden and has to be found through well thought-out questioning.

How to play: each student puts 2 objects on his/her desk (for example a pencil and a diary; or a pencil sharpener and a notebook etc) and nothing else. The objects should all be different. Each student names his/her 2 objects and, from his/her place, shows them to everyone. At this point one of the students is sent outside the classroom and, whilst he/she is outside, the others decide upon the object to guess, for example "the pencil". The owner of the pencil takes it off his/her desk and all other players must also remove one object of their choosing from their desks and they should be hidden in bags or under desks.

The player outside the class returns to the room and may walk around the desks but without touching anything or looking under desks or in bags. He/she then picks 3 classmates and asks them 1-3 questions (based on the age of the players) about the physical characteristics of the object to which the answer can only be "YES", "NO", or "I DON'T KNOW".

Based on these answers he/she must try to guess the object chosen by the class. If he/she correctly guesses the object he/he then chooses the next person to leave the class for another round. Naturally everyone returns their 2 objects to their desks and chooses different objects for the next round.

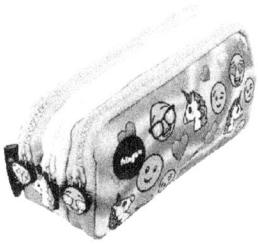

THE GRANDPARENTS' DINNER

Materials: A3 paper, coloured paper, a publicity leaflet from a supermarket etc, scissors, paper glue.

Background: in pairs players pretend to be 2 siblings who must do the shopping for their grandparents. The winner is the couple who create the best dinner!

How to play: players get into pairs sitting next to one another. The supervisor gives each pair a piece of A3 paper and one of the supermarket leaflets (which should be easily available in the necessary number) and gives the instructions: each pair must, within a set time, do the shopping for a complete dinner for the teacher's parents (or grandparents who no-one knows! The supervisor should establish that the 2 imaginary elderly people don't have any health problems or food intolerances). This should be done by choosing products from the leaflet (then cutting them out and sticking on the A3 sheet) but without spending more than 40 euros.

Students use scissors and glue. Food and objects should be cut out and glued onto the paper complete with the price. The supervisor should also point out that these grandparents don't have any other useful foodstuffs in their house at the moment. The players can take on different roles within their pair.

Once completed the A3 sheets are stuck on the wall so everyone can see. Together they look at their classmates work and also check that they haven't spent more than 40 euros. They should also check that the shopping contains all the necessary ingredients (for example: if they have bought salad, they should also have bought oil and salt! If they have bought coffee, they should also have bought sugar!).

If they have forgotten a vital ingredient the supervisor adds it to the sheet with a marker pen.

At the end of the game all competitors who haven't exceeded the 40 euros limit and who have bought all the necessary ingredients are praised.

15.01.2021

15.01

THE DIVISION CHALLENGE

Materials: 2 sets of identical pieces of papers (about 15cm x 15cm) in 2 different colours. Each set should have the same number of pieces, chosen by the supervisor based on the age and level of the players. Each player receives one piece of paper. (You can use playing cards if you don't have more than 10 players).

Background: this is a game to repeat and revise mental arithmetic. Here we are using the concept of division but you can obviously use different functions such as odd and even numbers, addition, subtraction, multiplication, greater or less than etc.

How to play: if possible divide the class into two teams with an equal number of players. Children can stay at their own desks.

Let's imagine that in a class we have 2 teams of 9 players each. The numbers 2, 3, 4, 5, 6, 7, 8, 9, 10 are given out to each team.

The supervisor says a number and then counts to 3 or 5. All players who have a card which they think is a divider of that number should hold up their cards. So if the supervisor says the number 20, the players with cards 2, 4, and 5 from each team should hold their cards up. Beware: once a card has been held up players cannot change their mind.

After each turn the supervisor gives 1 point to each player who has correctly raised their card and records the points for each team. After each turn the points are added onto the previous ones. When the supervisor decides it is a good time the game stops and the total scores of both teams are compared.

Variation: for example for players aged 6/7 - THE ADDITION CHALLENGE. The supervisor says numbers which are the sum of 2 numbers on the assigned cards. Players should only raise their cards if both of the 2 numbers which can be added to make the total are in their team. For example, if the supervisor says 6 only players with cards 2 and 4 can raise their cards (5 can't because there isn't a number 1, 3 can't because there isn't another number 3 in their team); if the number 8 is said, four players can raise their cards: numbers 2 and 6, 3 and 5. Obviously you can use other variations.

For older students you could use THE MULTIPLICATION CHALLENGE. Use the cards 10, 12, 14, 15, 18, 20, 21, 24, 25. In this case the supervisor says "multiples of 2!" or "multiples of 3!" or "multiples of 4!" etc. If the supervisor says "multiples of 18!" only the player with card 18 can raise their card, in the case of "multiples of 11!" no-one can.

IMPORTANT THINGS

Materials: 4 pieces of paper and large felt tips.

Background: all students work together to create a code of "good behaviour" in class to help everyone to respect each other.

How to play: each student can remain sitting in his/her place. This game has the same characteristics as the so-called "welcome or getting to know you" games and is a useful resource for new groups as a kind of "pact" between the members of the group.

The supervisor explains that if any group wants to work together for a period of time, its members would benefit from establishing ideas, aims and ways to best work harmoniously together.

The supervisor hands out 2 pre-prepared pieces of paper entitled "important things for me" and "important things to get on well with my classmates".

Each participant is invited to give his/her opinion or idea in both categories. Once this phase has finished the supervisor asks everyone to give a mark to each suggestion: one by one the ideas are read out and each student gives a mark from 1 (to vote participants raise their hand and use their fingers to vote). The total score from each vote is written on the big piece of paper.

Once this phase has finished the supervisor transfers the ideas in descending order of preference based on their scores onto the other 2 big pieces of paper which have got the same titles.

In this way the group will establish a set of rules to "work together as a group according to the needs of the individual" which can be used a later date to reflect upon briefly or in greater detail.

The 2 big pieces of paper will provide a frame of reference for the group for the entire time they work together and it should soon become clear that in order to "get important things done" whilst respecting everyone's individual rights and sharing those principles, a set of rules about common behaviour and rights must be established and adhered to.

SPEAK AND LISTEN	**SHARE FEELINGS**
BE NICE TO EACH OTHER	**NO HITTING**
DON'T SWEAR	**BE KIND**
PLAY TOGETHER NICELY	**HELP EACH OTHER**
DON'T ARGUE	**RESPECT EACH OTHER**

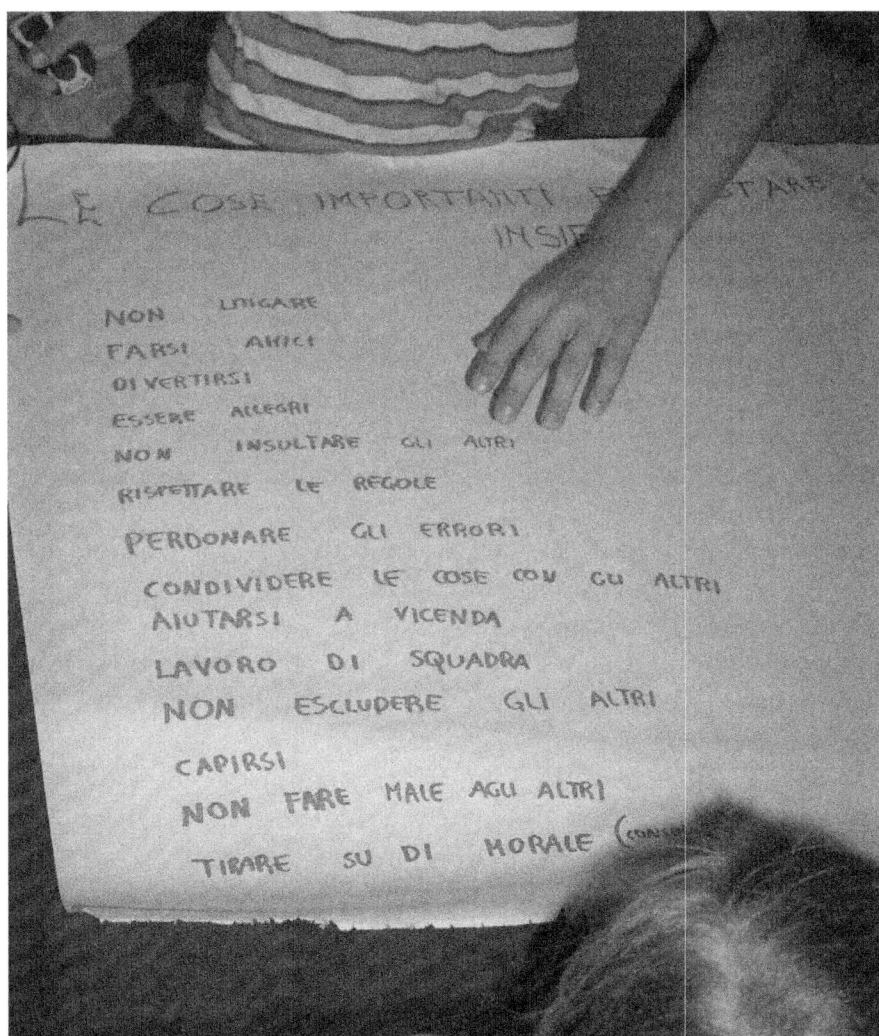

TEAM HANGMAN

Materials: a blackboard and chalk or a big piece of paper and a marker pen; 2 sheets of A4 paper.

Background: players must try to guess a word with a limited number of attempts having only been given the first and last letters, which is illustrated by the gradual construction of a "hangman".

How to play: a group or class of children is divided into 2 teams (with for example 10 players on each team). Each group chooses 10 words (with a maximum of 12 letters) to be guessed by the other team and one of the team members writes them down on the piece of paper and gives the paper to the supervisor.

One player from the first team draws a gallows on the big piece of paper and underneath a dashed line with as many dashes as there are letters of the chosen word and writes in the first and last letter.

A player from the second team says one letter at a time in an attempt to guess the mystery word and, if the letter is in the word it is written on the correct dash. If it is not in the mystery word, the player at the board draws part of the hanged man's body in 5 steps: head, body, arm, arm, leg, leg (possibly 7 for younger children by adding the 2 hands together and then the 2 feet).

Players win by guessing the word before the hanged man is completed. When all players have had a go, the winning players are counted up.

Beware: each player has only 2 attempts to guess the word without being given clues by his/her teammates.

You can also use group or individual scores. For individual scores: if a player guesses the word without ever having given a wrong letter he/she receives 0 penalty points, if he/she guesses the word but has given 3 incorrect letters he/she receives 3 points and so on. If he/she doesn't guess the word or gives 5 incorrect letters or guesses the complete word incorrectly twice he/she receives the maximum number of points (5 or 7).

Team game: the total of the individual points. The winning team is the one who gets the lowest score.

THE INTERVIEW

Materials: no materials needed. You can use a piece of A4 paper and a pencil for every player.

Background: players try to guess the identity of a mystery person as the supervisor and another player "act out" an interview in the style of a journalist and the mystery person.

How to play: the game can be played in a small group sitting in a circle or in the classroom with players sitting at their desks.

Each player takes it in turns to imitate a mystery person given to him/her by the supervisor (or chosen by the player him/herself): the star of a well-known animated film and/or a fairy tale, a TV personality or someone from the world of sport or show-business, a famous historical person or a living person known to the whole group etc.

The identity of the person is, for the moment, only known to the supervisor and the chosen player. The 2 sit the correct distance apart, in full view of each other and start to chat. The adult asks questions ("have you been in an animated film?", "are you a sportsperson?", "when we see you how are you dressed?", "are you alive?", "do you appear in our school books?", "have you appeared on TV?", "what colour is your skin?", "do you live in our city?" etc) and the child, imitating the mystery person, responds without revealing his/her identity. If he/she doesn't know the answer to one of the questions he/she can avoid embarrassment by saying "I'm sorry but I don't remember!"

As soon as one of the other players listening to the interview thinks they have guessed the identity of the mystery person they raise their hand and are asked by the supervisor to reveal the name of the mystery person. Beware: if someone guesses the name of the mystery person incorrectly, he/she can no longer participate during this interview.

Variation: the format of the game can be used to guess a mystery animal. The interview can also last for a certain time set by the supervisor and at the end players have to write the name of the person on a piece of paper. The papers are collected and the name revealed and all those who correctly guessed the person win a point.

NAME, OBJECT, PLACE

Materials: an A4 piece of paper and a pen for each player.

Background: under the pressure of a time limit which isn't set but is different every time, players try to find unusual words to fit into different categories.

How to play: this is a timed game which can be repeated as many times as you like. Each player is given a piece of paper and a pen and draws a grid with as many columns as categories you want to use: names of people, things, cities, animals, vegetables, rivers-lakes-seas, jobs, verbs, colours, clothes, toys etc. The last column on the right is to keep score and is entitled "total points per row or TPR". The rows on the grid will fill up with each round played.

The supervisor, or one player at a time, says a letter which will be the first letter of every word in each column. When the time has run out (or when a player raises his/her hand to say that they have completed every column) each child records his/her points in each box as the words are marked:

3 points for a correct word and if all the other players haven't managed to find a word for this category;

2 points when the word is correct and no-one else has written the same word;

1 point if the word is correct but other players have also written the same word;

0 points if the box is blank.

The total points for each row should be recorded in the last column on the right (TPR).

It is important to clarify certain points before starting the game. For example: "names" can only be names of people in use in Italy....or not; "city".....only Italian cities are valid, or European cities or cities of the world, for "things" we mean objects (foods, parts and organs of the body, organic and vegetable matter won't be accepted), "Jack and Jackie" are the same name (1 point) and the same goes for "dog and dogs"(1 point) and "I write, they write and to write" (1 point) etc.

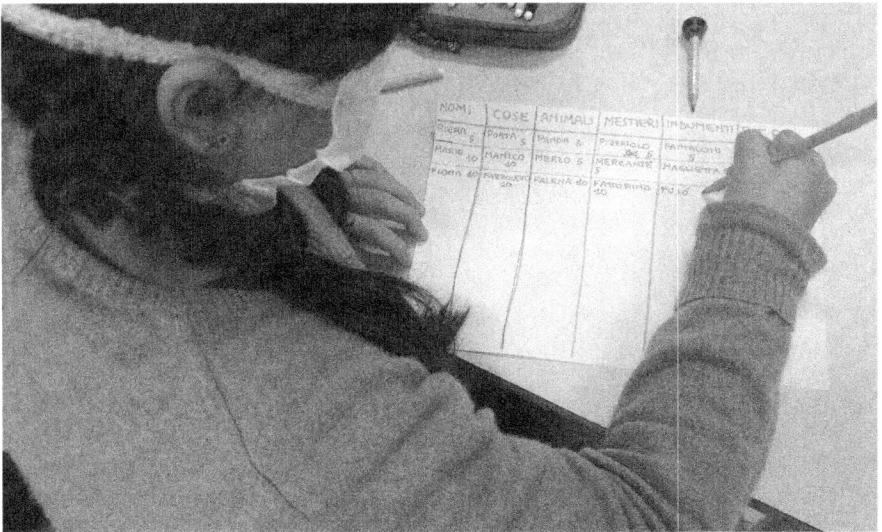

ARITHMETIC OLYMPICS

Materials: 2 boards or 2 big pieces of paper hung on the wall: chalk or a marker pen for each child.

Background: 2 teams challenge each others' maths skills in the arithmetic Olympics.

How to play: if possible divide the class into two teams. The students on the left half are the first team and those on the right the second.

The supervisor draws on the 2 boards (or pieces of paper) 2 identical rectangles or tables of addition (or subtraction, multiplication or division – based on the age and skills of the students).

Players from each team are given a number (as in the game with the handkerchief or flag stealing). Every team will therefore have a player number 1, 2 etc.

On the supervisor's signal each player number 1 goes to his/her table and puts in the result of the sum (only one) in a square of their choice. Once done, he/she returns to his/her place and as soon as he/she is sitting down, player number 2 can start, then number 3 etc.

When all players have had a go the turns start again until all the table has been completed.

The first team to complete the table stops the game. The tables are checked and the winner declared.

HIDDEN WORD OR FIND THE VERB

Materials: one book per player, for example a school text book.

Background: players must guess a certain word within a text using clues given by the supervisor.

How to play: players can remain in their own places. They are asked to read the chosen text and, once finished, the supervisor gives different clues (think of crossword clues) to guess a word and then to find it within the text.

For example, in a text about summer holidays, the supervisor wants players to guess the word "sea". He/she has got many ways to help them guess, based on the age and skills of the players:

1) 3 letters, begins with an S and finishes with an A

2) It evaporates and becomes clouds

3) You can dive into it

4) It's an anagram of ESA

5) It's AES backwards

6) It's used by ships

7) Plankton like it etc.

The player who finds the word in the text, circles it and puts up his/her hand. He/she must read the sentence containing the word to confirm if the answer is correct and, if it is, he/she is awarded a point. At the end of the game the person with the most points is congratulated as the winner.

Variation: the same game can be played in teams. If possible divide the room into 4 quarters and those in each quarter form a team. Each individual player's points are added to the team total.

Other variations: the supervisor writes on the board or paper the words he/she wants the players to guess. He/she then sets a time limit and each player must find and highlight as many of the words as possible. When the time limit is up each individual player's points are counted and added to the team total. In this variation the supervisor can choose words which are repeated in the text and each time that the word is highlighted it scores a point.

FREE WORDS

Materials: a pencil and paper for each player.

Background: players try to complete a composition using a series of given letters.

How to play: the supervisor says 10/15 letters (a mix of vowels and consonants) or writes them on the board or sheet of paper hung on the wall.

In a set time each players tries to make as many words as possible (with minimum of 5 letters) using those letters (the letters may be reused in new words but cannot be used twice in the same word).

When the time is up the words are checked. 1point is given to whoever has written the most words and 1 point is given to whoever has written the longest word (there can be more than 1 player for both categories). After a few rounds the first player to reach 5/10 points is declared the winner of "Free words".

FORBIDDEN WORDS

Materials: pencil and paper or crayons and felt-tips.

Background: players take it in turns to help their teammates to guess a word within a set time limit but they must do so without saying the actual words or other associated words.

How to set up the game: players can remain at their desks to play. Starting from one side of the room and working across, players are numbered in order and must remember their number in relation to those either side of them.

How to play: the supervisor should have prepared sheets of paper with a word written in pencil and underlined, for example TABLE. This will be the word to be guessed by the group. Under the word TABLE are written 4 or 5 "forbidden" words (in this case for example WOOD, LEGS, KITCHEN, CHAIRS, EAT). Players take it turns to be the person who describes the word given by the supervisor. They cannot use any of the 4 or 5 forbidden words (or derivatives of those words) and if they do, their turn will be invalid and a new player with a new word will take their place. The aim of the game is to guess a certain number of words (for example in a group of 15 students they could guess 20 out of 40 words) in a set time. The number of words and time limit can change according to the age and linguistic skills of the players, their familiarity with and enthusiasm for repeating the game. The supervisor can make the game progressively more difficult by, for example, using more and more complex words or shortening the time limit each round (for example the first time students have 20 minutes, the second 18, then 15 etc.).

Note: since players frequently use the forbidden words by accident and so pass onto a new word, the supervisor should prepare more "word cards with forbidden words" than the maximum numbers of words to be guessed.

Variation: the game can be played as a competition between 2 teams. In this case each team takes a turn to guess the word being described by one of their team. Each word correctly guessed wins a point. With children aged 9-11 we suggest that they should prepare the word cards at the beginning of the game with the word to be guessed and the forbidden words.

Each player from each team should get 2/4 sheets of paper and should write the chosen word (in green for example) and the forbidden words (in red for example). Once the preparation has been completed, the words from each team are given to the other team by the supervisor.

You could also propose categories for each round such as animals, school objects, sport etc.

TAVOLO

CUCINA
GAMBE
LEGNO
MANGIARE
QUATTRO

PASS THE PAPER

Materials: 2 sheets of paper for each pupil (only give 1 sheet to the last pupil of each team). A clear plastic cup for each team.

Background: pupils sit at their desks and each row of students forms a team. They complete challenges of manual speed and dexterity.

How to play: students sit at their desks in 4/6 parallel rows. Each row is a team. Before starting the game, each player (except one from each row) folds one of the sheets supplied into eight equal rectangles (three folds are enough to do this), tears the eight rectangles into pieces and scrunches them up into eight small balls of paper. The other sheet will be used to pass the balls.

At the one end of each row (it doesn't matter which end) the last player, who did not produce any balls, will be given the cup.

When the supervisor starts the game, the player at the first end of the row puts a ball onto the "ball passer" sheet of paper and passes it to the next player in the row who takes it with his/her "ball passer". He/she then adds one of his/her own balls and passes both of them to the next player and so on. This continues until the last player who, with all the balls on his/her "ball passer" transfers them into the cup without touching it. At the same time the first player has already started passing the second ball along the row and so it continues for 8 goes. Beware: every ball that falls off the "ball passer" cannot be picked up and put back in the game.

There are therefore 2 aims of the game: to be the first team to finish moving all the balls and secondly to get the most number of balls in the cup. So at the end of the game you can have two winning teams rather than just one.

MUTE PAINTER

Materials: blackboard and chalk, or big sheets of paper to stick on the wall and marker pens.

Background: one player pretends to be a mute painter who, to express him/herself, uses his/her talent.

How to play: one child at a time takes on the role of the mute painter who wants to communicate through drawing a picture. The other players can remain at their desks to play. They must try to guess 2 words (an adjective and noun) or a brief phrase which the supervisor has given to the child-painter, based on the age and abilities of the players. The first person to guess gets a point. At the end of the game (which lasts until each child has had a go at being the painter) the person with the most points is congratulated.

If using brief phrases it is a good idea to tell players how many words make up the phrase.

POINT THE FINGER

Materials: none needed.

Background: this is a game of attention and memory where players must quickly guess and indicate an object.

How to play: in a room which the children use often such as their classroom, the science laboratory or the school library (or you can also play in the garden or park), players stand in a circle (or at their desks). The supervisor says an object in the classroom and the player who points at the object first receives a point (2 or more children can also be given a point if they have all pointed at the same time).

The player who reaches 10 points first can be crowned champion of "point the finger".

Beware: if the game is repeated a few days later it would be a good idea to move as many objects around as possible before the players arrive.

FRUTTA E VERDURA DI STAGIONE
INVERNO

JAN. FEB. MAR. APR. MAY JUNE
JULY AUG. SEP. OCT. NOV. DEC.
SUN MON TUE WED THU FRI SAT
1 2 3 4 5 6 7
8 9 10 11 12 13 14
15 16 17 18 19 20 21
22 23 24 25 26 27 28
29 30 31

SHERLOCK HOLMES

Materials: everyday objects given to the students.

Background: someone has reported the theft of their valuables but, in fact, the theft never happened: it was made up to trick the insurance company to pay out the cost of the stolen objects. The skilled Sherlock Holmes has been brought in to track down the stolen goods.

How to play: players stay at their desks for the entirety of the game. Each player receives 5/10 objects from the supervisor which they put on their desks (not more than one of the same type of object). So on one desk for example there could be a book, a notebook, a pencil, a packet of tissues and a pencil sharpener. On another there could be scissors, a pair of glasses, a rubber, a book, a piece of paper, a pencil sharpener, a pen and a packet of tissues. In each round a child is chosen to take on the role of the famous imaginary English detective and he/she goes out of the room while the game is prepared but, before going out, he/she carefully inspects the desks and tries to memorise what objects are on them.

When he/she has left, the group selects the person to be the "rich fraudster". This player then chooses 3 objects from his/her desk and puts them on different desks of his/her classmates and then goes back to his/her place.

When the inspector returns, he/she walks among the desks and firstly tries to guess which one has been robbed. He/she has 3 tries to guess the victim of the theft and if incorrect, the game starts again with a different child as Sherlock Holmes. If he/she is correct, the victim names the 3 objects which have been stolen (for example a pencil, a book and a rubber) without describing them. At this point the investigator must walk among the desks and try to guess which they are (he/she has 6 goes to do this). No-one must touch the objects on their desks and when the 3 objects have been identified, their owner (the same person who moved them) goes to collect them.

Beware: this kind of game is easiest amongst groups who see each other every day and know what objects their classmates have (a certain kind of sharpener or a strange pencil, a book with particular cover etc). Otherwise it can be too difficult and players rarely guess correctly.

YES OR NO?

Materials: 2 pieces of paper of the same colour for half the class and 2 pieces of paper of another colour for the other half of the class: a felt-tip for each player.

Background: players try to answer questions as fast as possible. This kind of game can be a done with fun, amusing questions but can also be a way to revise and repeat topics studied within class. The questions can be asked by the supervisor or by a student.

How to play: ideally divide the room into 2. The players on the left hand side of the room (team one) each get 2 pieces of white paper. Those on the right (team 2) get 2 pieces of yellow paper (or another colour). Everybody writes YES on one piece of paper and NO on the other.

The supervisor writes 2 columns or rows on the board to keep score. He/she then asks questions about a specific subject (eg the ancient Egyptians, cities and regions of Britain or science and natural phenomena etc). Whoever knows the answer must hold up the correct piece of paper. The first player to hold up the correct answer wins a point for his/her team. He/she then puts that piece of paper away (in his/her desk or in a book) and can't use it again (until a new round of the game starts). If the answer is incorrect the team loses a point. Each player can therefore only respond twice.

The first team to be left with no pieces of paper (with YES or NO) stops the game and the scores are counted.

RHYTHMIC BINGO

Materials: a songsheet for every song for each player prepared by the supervisor, 8 different small objects taken from a pencilcase.

Background: using the game of bingo as a framework, many other variations can be invented to be played in the classroom (which are suitable for the age and level of the students). Bingo with maths sums, bingo with grammar and the variation which we present here as an example. The cards can be quickly prepared by dividing sheets of paper into 8 sections and filling them in with 8 numbers or 8 words or musical notes chosen from a list which have been written on a large piece of paper.

How to play: players can stay at their desks to play. The supervisor claps his/her hands or uses a drum or tambourine to give a random series of musical notes taken from the large list. If players have one of the notes on their card they cover the square in which it is written with one of their 8 objects (a rubber, a sharpener, a pen top etc.).

12.02.2021

12.02.2021

AUCTION

Materials: papers and felt-tips pens. A supermarket leaflet for the supervisor.

Background: a type of auction where every team bids for an object and those who come closest to the actual value are the winners. Any bids over the value won't be counted.

How to play: players can stay at their desks. If possible divide the room into 4 parts and so form 4 teams.

For example, with a class of 16 students there would be 4 teams of 4 players. Each player divides his/her sheet into 4 parts and draws an object (given by the supervisor) in each part. Each team will therefore draw the same 16 everyday objects randomly chosen by the supervisor from a leaflet from a supermarket. When the pictures are finished the "silent auction" starts and each group decides how much each object should cost (without being heard by the other teams) and writes the number next to the relevant drawing. Players should keep the appropriate distance but the desks can be set up so that team member are facing each other). When all the groups have completed this stage the supervisor states the names of the objects in turn to find which team has got closest to the actual value of the object on the leaflet. This group is "awarded" the item and marks it on their sheet.

Note: based on the age and number of players, the number of students in each team may vary and therefore so may the number of objects and the number of sections that each sheet of paper is divided into.

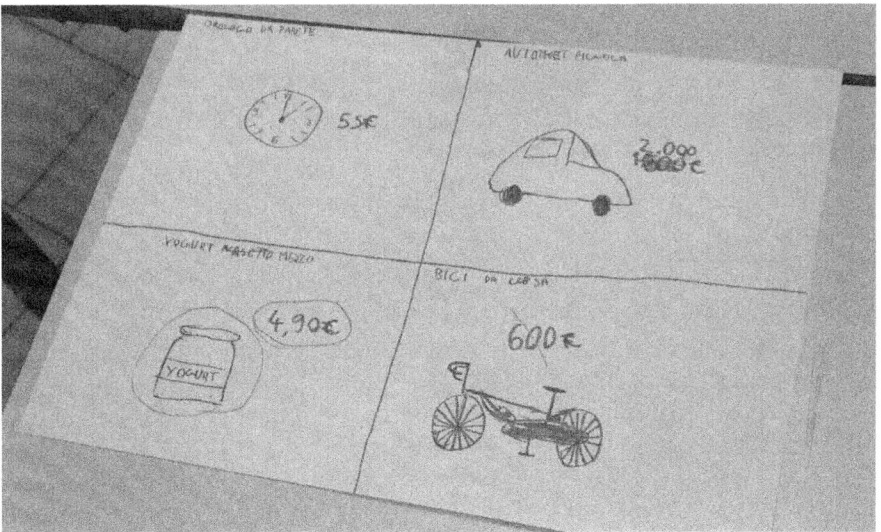

FULL SCHOOLBAG

Materials: a red card (OUT) and a green card (IN) for every player. The supervisor needs some pieces of paper and a pen.

Background: players stay in their places and compete 4 at a time (or 3 depending on the number of players) against each other.

How to play: the children stay at their desks. Everyone puts out the green card (IN PLAY). The supervisor picks the first player who then chooses who he/she wants to play against. Those 4 players stand up next to their desks ready to play:

first player – "in my bag I've got… a book";

second player – "in my bag I've got… a book and a pencil case";

third player – "in my bag I've got… a book, a pencil case and a notebook";

fourth player – "in my bag I've got… a book, a pencil case, a notebook and a snack".

Then the first player starts again and continues to add objects to the list – "in my bag I've got… a book, a pencil case, a notebook, a snack and a cap" etc.

Play continues adding objects to the list which players must repeat every time with the objects in the correct order. If anyone gets the order wrong or misses an object they have to sit down and change their green card for a red one (and can't take part in this round again). The other players continue until 1 player is left standing with his/her green card on display. Then the next round can start with the next 4 players.

According to the number of players the last round can be a challenge between 2,3 or 4 players. This will also be determined by how many times players who won their first round are called to play again (since with the green card displayed they be called to play again in the round immediately after).

NELLO ZAINO HO MESSO IL DIARIO, IL PORTAPENNE, IL QUADERNO, LA MERENDA, LA CARTELLINA E LE FIGURINE...

*"Thank you for reading this book.
If you enjoyed it please visit the site where
you purchased it and write a brief review.
Your feedback is important to me and will
help other readers decide whether to read
the book too.*

Thank you!".

Paolo Macagno

By the same author on Amazon you can find
**"SOCIALLY DISTANCED GAMES
WITH NO CONTACT"**

Printed in Great Britain
by Amazon